Serial Killers Encyclopedia

The Book Of The World's Worst Murderers In History

by Martin G. Welsh

Descrierea CIP a Bibliotecii Naționale a României
MARTIN G. WELSH
   Serial Killers Encyclopedia. The Book Of The World's Worst Murderers In History/ by Martin G. Welsh. - București : My Ebook, 2018
   ISBN 978-606-983-592-0

94
316

Serial Killers Encyclopedia

The Book Of The World's Worst Murderers In History

By Martin G. Welsh

My Ebook Publishing House
Bucharest, 2018

CONTENTS

CHAPTER ONE: **THE GENESIS**	13
CHAPTER TWO: **THE CRIMSON COUNTESS**	17
CHAPTER THREE: **THE SAVVY SOCIOPATH**	21
CHAPTER FOUR: **THE CAREFUL CARETAKER**	25
CHAPTER FIVE: **THE POGO PIPER**	29
CHAPTER SIX: **THE SOUTHERN SAVAGE**	34
CHAPTER SEVEN: **THE FAMILY THAT KILLS TOGETHER, STAYS TOGETHER**	38
CHAPTER EIGHT: **THE NEFARIOUS NANNY**	43
CHAPTER NINE: **THE MONSTER KILLER OF CHINA**	47
CHAPTER TEN: **THE RED RIPPER**	50
Conclusion	55

INTRODUCTION

I want to thank and congratulate you for buying this book, *"The Book Of Serial Killers: The World's Worst Murderers."* This book contains pertinent information about the world's most notorious serial killers.

You will find out all you wanted to know about some of the world's complex and most evil minds. It details their grisly acts and tells their stories. It is not for the faint of heart. Murder, mayhem and the macabre make this read a morbidly fascinating ride. Enjoy and don't read in the dark.

Copyright 2018 by Zen Mastery - All rights reserved

This document is geared towards providing exact and reliable information in regards to the topic and issue covered. The publication is sold with the idea that the publisher is not required to render accounting, officially permitted, or otherwise, qualified services. If advice is necessary, legal or professional, a practiced individual in the profession should be ordered.

- From a Declaration of Principles which was accepted and approved equally by a Committee of the American Bar Association and a Committee of Publishers and Associations.

In no way is it legal to reproduce, duplicate, or transmit any part of this document in either electronic means or in printed format. Recording of this publication is strictly prohibited and any storage of this document is not allowed unless with written permission from the publisher. All rights reserved.

The information provided herein is stated to be truthful and consistent, in that any liability, in terms of inattention or otherwise, by any usage or abuse of any policies, processes, or directions contained within is the solitary and utter responsibility of the recipient reader. Under no circumstances will any legal responsibility or blame be held against the publisher for any reparation, damages, or monetary loss due to the information herein, either directly or indirectly.

Respective authors own all copyrights not held by the publisher.

The information herein is offered for informational purposes solely, and is universal as so. The presentation of the information is without contract or any type of guarantee assurance.

The trademarks that are used are without any consent, and the publication of the trademark is without permission or backing by the trademark owner. All trademarks and brands within this book are for clarifying purposes only and are the owned by the owners themselves, not affiliated with this document.

CHAPTER ONE: THE GENESIS

Picture this. East End London's white Chapel in the 1800s, teeming with immigrants and poverty. Filled with the desperate and the damned. With the surge in the population, East End became over crowded with poor working and housing conditions. With poverty and starvation imminent, most women were driven to prostitution. A place like that is the perfect melting pot to create one of the most prolific serial killers of all time. The most unsettling part? They were never caught.

In 1888, Jack the Ripper terrorized the streets and slums of Whitechapel killing prostitutes, dumping their mutilated bodies and confounding the police. He has many suspected victims. The time of the murders multiple attacks were recorded in the Whitechapel environs and were collated by the police, collectively known as "The Whitechapel Murders." Though there is the uncertainty of how many lives the Ripper claimed exactly, five have been definitively linked and are widely believed to have been victims of the same killer.

The first victim was Mary Ann Nichols. Her body was found at around 3:42 am with two cuts on her throat, and her abdomen partially ripped open. There were other wounds on her abdomen caused by the same knife.

The second victim, Annie Chapman was found near a door way. As with the first victim, her throat was slashed twice. Unlike the first, her abdomen was ripped entirely open with her uterus removed. Her body was found by 6 am on 8th September 1888. Witness account placed her with a gentleman at around 5:30 am.

The third and fourth victims, Elizabeth Stride and Catherine Eddowes were found on the same day. It is speculated by some that The Ripper was interrupted during the murder of Stride, while others argue whether or not she was actually a victim of the Ripper at all. Both were killed on the 30th of September with Stride's body discovered at around 1 am. It was found with one cut severing the artery with no abdominal mutilation. Eddowes' body was found about 45 minutes afterwards with a mutilated abdomen, deep slashes in her throat and part of her left kidney and uterus missing.

The fifth victim was Mary Jane Kelly. Her mutilated body was found in her house at 10:45 am on 9th November 1888. Most of her organs and her heart were missing.

The nature of the crimes were grisly and shocking, creating a massive media sensation at the time. Though a lot of suspects were arrested, none of them was tried. The information about the murders today is a mixture of fact, conjectures, opinions and sensational media stories. The killer was never found. Today, the motive remains a mystery left to speculation. The Ripper is so fascinating that there is a term coined for the study and analysis of the murders, Ripperology. Among the highly fascinating serial killers in history and the identity remains a mystery.

CHAPTER TWO: THE CRIMSON COUNTESS

No serial killer list would be complete without the addition of this notorious countess. In brutality and body count she remains notable. Countess Elizabeth Báthory de Ecsed was a Hungarian Noble and alleged murderer of over 650 people. So incredible is her body count that the Guinness book of records has accorded her the infamous honor of the most prolific female serial killer of all time.

With her wealth and nobility, she could have gotten away with almost anything. Yet, the extent of her crimes was too much to ignore. With four other conspirators, over three hundred witness testimonies, physical evidence, actual victims, it is difficult to argue that The Bloody Countess was as sadistic as they come.

She lured girls with the promise of work at her Castle. When that ruse stopped working, she began to kill the daughters of lesser gentry who were sent to her gynaeceum to learn etiquette. Her method of killing? Torture. There are multiple accounts of her beating, starving, freezing and burning victims. There were reports that she bit off flesh from the faces and arms of the victims. Some reports have her scalding the girls with hot tongs and putting them in freezing water. There were also reports that she drained her victims of blood, especially the young girls and bathed in their blood. She believed it would make her younger. There was a prevailing belief then that the blood or bodily fluids of the young would transfer their health and vitality to any one who ingested them. The Bloody Countess was also suspected of cannibalism.

When reports got too much to ignore an investigation was launched. A delegation was sent to her Castle and they caught her red-handed. Inside the castle was the body of a girl and another was dying. Victims remains were removed from the grounds of the buildings, some of them still in chains. Considering her social standing at the time the death penalty was considered too scandalous. She was sentenced to house arrest. Left alone in a bricked up room where she died four years later. Her burial place to this day is unknown.

You would think for someone who committed such heinous crime a fate worse than spending your last days in a cushy Castle, even without the option of leaving would be too lenient. You would be right, but that doesn't change the fact that it is exactly how the bloody countess spent the last of her days. Sometimes justice doesn't seem to serve it's course.

CHAPTER THREE: THE SAVVY SOCIOPATH

Handsome, brilliant and charismatic. Sounds like a front runner for the most eligible bachelor of the year, right? This was also the description most of his friends gave one of the most prolific serial killers in recent history. A picture of him had ladies swooning and lining up, long after the extent of his crimes were exposed. He was Theodore Robert Bundy.

During his earlier years, he studied law before dropping out, was highly respected in some political circles and even worked for an organization that helped find missing women. Ironic, isn't it? During these times he assaulted, raped and murdered women. Worse yet? He returned to the crime scenes to sexually assault their bodies until putrefaction made it impossible. The method he uses to kill, he prefers either strangulation or blunt force trauma, both were silent methods of killing. At first, he broke into houses and attacked his sleeping victims, bludgeoning them to death. Later on, he refined his method of operation often coming up with ruses that made him look either injured or like an authority figure. On many occassions, he will wear a plaster cast on his leg or put his arm in a sling. He used crutches, mimicked someone who was injured, to lull his victims into a false sense of security.

Though Ted was interviewed by top most Psychologists, it was difficult to pin point exactly what his disorder was. The closest was that he exhibited many personality traits of those suffering from Anti-Social Personality Disorder, commonly known as Psychopathy or Sociopathy. He displayed multiple sociopathic tendencies such as shallow charm, an understanding of right and wrong with little effect on behaviour, manipulative behaviour, narcissism, etc. He blamed the extent of his crimes on violent pornography. He was quoted in an interview saying

"My experience with ... pornography that deals on a violent level with sexuality, is once you become addicted to it ... I would keep looking for more potent, more explicit, more graphic kinds of material. Until you reach a point where the pornography only goes so far ... where you begin to wonder if maybe actually doing it would give that which is beyond just reading it or looking at it."

Most of the psychiatrists that interviewed him were of the opinion that his attempt to blame porn was another manipulative machination. Ted Bundy confessed to about thirty homicides, but it is suspected that he committed more. He was deliberately cryptic about the location of most of his victims, some of which were never found. He is also a suspect in multiple homicides and may likely be never identified as the killer.

Bundy was sentenced to death and finally executed after all the appeal options had been exhausted. In his final months, with nothing left to live for, he stopped protesting his innocence and confessed the gruesome nature of his crimes. His was killed on the 24th of January 1989 at age 49. He was electrocuted.

Chapter Four: The Careful Caretaker

There is virtually nothing more soothing or comforting than being in the hands of an experienced medical practitioner. It is almost instinctive to trust them with our wellbeing and health. After all, they know best, they know exactly what they are doing. They will give us the best care we require, even if it kills them or us.

Harold Shipman is one such medical practitioner. He is in this book because he not only abused his uniquely privileged position of almost instant trust, he also got away with it long enough to murder more than 250 victims over a period of twenty three years. In Shipman's case, the doctor targeted older victims with his youngest victim being a 42 year old man. In his early years, he was close to his mother who died of lung cancer. During the final stages of her cancer, she was often administered morphine which helped with the pain. Psychologist believe that this created and indelible mark on his psyche. His murder weapon was an over dosage of diamorphine. After the deaths he would alter and forge medical records making up stories of ill health for his victims. He often signed a cremation form, further hiding his crimes. Under his care about 459 patients died over the course of his career. It is not clear how many of those were from natural causes and how many were victims of murder.

After the extent of his crimes was discovered, there was a re-examination of medical practices in Britain. He was also suspected of burglary with around 66 pieces of jewellery found in his garage in 1998. There was an inquiry named "The Shipman Inquiry" that was set up to investigate the actual depth of Shipman's crimes. The head of the Council could only link him to 215 deaths though there were "Strong suspicions" of more. His victims were mostly elderly women in good health.

He was charged to court and found guilty of fifteen counts of murder. The other murder charges were never brought up because of public uproar over the killings. It was considered that having a fair hearing after the news of his previous conviction broke would be impossible.

He died on the 24th of January 2004 in prison by tying his bed sheet to the window and making a noose out of it. He hung himself He was 57 at the time of his death, just a day before his 58th birthday. He never actually confessed to the murders even though there was ample evidence linking him. The families of the deceased feel cheated. There was no acceptance of guilt on his part and whether or not he was remorseful is a secret the good doctor took to his grave.

The good doctor, not only managed to unsettle us with his unique brand of care, he managed to force the entire medical structure of Britain's health sysyem to improve. Ironically because of this, the system changed for the better. Or at least we can hope so.

CHAPTER FIVE: THE POGO PIPER

An upstanding citizen, a successful business owner, respected member of society and charitable human to boot. If this description sounds too good to be true, it's because it is. John Wayne Gacy was all of those things; he was also a vicious serial killer who murdered as many as 33 men and buried them in the crawl space.

Gacy had an early troubled life. His father was abusive, constantly belittling him. By Gacy's own account one of his earliest memories was of his father beating him with a leather belt. The situation escalated for Gacy as he was reportedly sexually assaulted by a family friend who was a contractor. The man took him on rides outside the house and fondled him. Gacy never told his father who already believed him to be a "Sissy" because he was afraid his father would blame him. The rift between his father and him eventually drove him to Nevada where he found a job as a mortician's assistant. It was on this job, that he found himself climbing into a coffin and cuddling a teenage male body. The even scared him so much that he went back home.

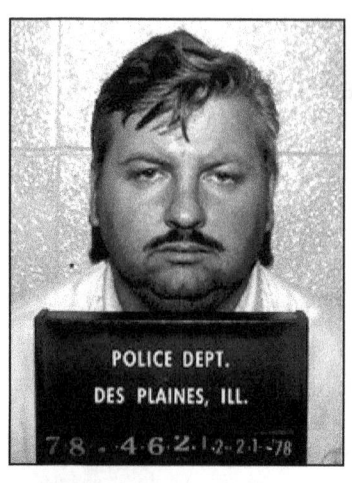

He was arrested for assault multiple times but finally seemed to straighten his life. He became a celebrated member of the society and often dressed as Pogo the clown or Patches the clown, to perform at charity functions. Successful both in business and in community standing, it seemed he had turned around his life and had nowhere to go but up.

Then on January 2nd 1972 Gacy's picked up his first victim Timothy Jack McCoy. Allegedly, after a night of sightseeing Gacy woke up to find McCoy standing at the entrance of his bedroom with a knife. There was a scuffle, Gacy ended up stabbing him multiple time, killing the boy. It wasn't until afterwards that Gacy noticed the makings of breakfast on the table with whole bacon yet to be sliced. McCoy had been preparing breakfast when he'd come to wake Gacy up. The entire attack had been a complete misunderstanding but by then it was already too late. Pogo the friendly clown had experienced the exhilarating rush of his first kill and like an addict, there was no going back.

While Gacy's business was growing, so was his body count. He lured countless men to his house, plied them with alcohol, tricked them into wearing handcuffs, then raped and strangled them with a tourniquet. He buried most of the bodies in the crawl space while dumping about five bodies in Des Plaines River. The police became suspicious after the disappearance of Robert Peist and kept constant surveillance on him. The surveillance wore Gacy down. Eventually, he broke and confessed to the murders. The entire community was in shock as body after body was pulled out of Gacy's crawl space.

He was sentenced to death. The execution sentence was carried out fourteen years later on May 9, 1994. His final spoken words were,

"Kiss my ass."

When next you get the urge to dismiss Stephen King's Cannibal clown, Pennywise as the workings of an over active imagination remembers Pogo.

Chapter Six: The Southern Savage

Moses Sithole is commonly referred to as the African Ted Bundy. A dubious honor at best but fitting to one of the most prolific serial killers to ever be found on the African Continent. Africa doesn't seem to have a very hight rate of serial killers. Mostly because of the notoriously shoddy and corrupt police workforce. Which is one of the many reasons why Sithole's case is memorable.

His early years were unstable. His father died when he was five. Afterwards, his mother abandoned his family leaving them in the care of an orphanage where he was allegedly mistreated.

He spent about seven years in prison. The time he blamed for twisting him into a murderer.

After he was released, he created a fake company and lured women to come in for interviews. When they came, he took them to an abandoned field where he would proceed to rape and strangle them in their own underwear. Afterwards, he would write bitch on their foreheads and dump their bodies. He killed more to thirty people. When he was sent to prison earlier in his life for assault, his girlfriend abandoned him. The rejection made him angry and he often credits the reason for his killings as that rejection. His First murders took place in Atteridgeville before he moved on to Boksburg and then Cleaveland. Which is where the moniker, the "ABC" killer was gotten from.

Eventually, he was linked to one of the victims after he was reportedly seen with her and claimed his motive was punishment for the unfair imprisonment. He blamed the women who accused him of rape, alleging that they lied. He maintained his innocence. He was caught and tried and was found guilty. Sithole has been given a sentence of 2410 years and has been ordered by a judge to serve at least 930 before he is considered for parole. A fitting punishment for one who held an entire country in the grips of fear. A person who Mandela himself had to calm the nation after he had caused such panic. Many of his neighbours couldn't have guessed that a killer was lurking in the guise of a mild, well mannered man. Underneath lurked pure evil. After the murders, Sithole usually called the family members of the victim to taunt them. Through that act, he showed a lack of remorse.

An inability to empathize with pain. During his DNA testing, it was discovered that he was HIV positive.

We often find that the worst monsters were not created from the dark depths of our worst imaginations. They are here, among us, blending in. Sithole is the perfect example that twisted individuals can spring up anywhere, not just in the urban jungles of the West.

Chapter Seven: The Family That Kills Together, Stays Together.

There are many fun family activities. A day at the amusement Park, dinner at McDonald's, a nice interesting family movie and if you belong to the Bender family, murdering several guests at the family owned Inn.

The Benders were John Snr(Pa) Bender, Elvira (Ma) Bender, John Jnr Bender and Kate Bender. The family settled in Labette County in Texas in 1870. Over the years, the Benders grew quite a reputation in the town. It was reported that Pa Bender spoke very little English and what English he did speak remained so garbled that no one could ever understand him. Ma Bender was so unfriendly and unwelcoming that she was called a she devil by her neighbours. John Jnr was known to smile at nothing all the time and was generally regarded as a half wit. While Kate Bender was beautiful and a self proclaimed psychic and clairvoyant. It is a source of debate as to whether the Kate and John Jnr Bender were brother and sister or man and wife through a common law marriage.

Along the trail that led westwards people began to disappear. Bodies were found. In May 1871 the body of a man known only as Jones was found in Drum Creek with his head caved in by a hammer and his throat slashed. Around February 1872 two more bodies were found with suspects arrested and nobody charged. The Benders reported lured travellers on the highway to dinner and rest at their house, putting the guest in a "special seat" at a position on the table. Kate Bender would then distract the hapless guest while one of the Bender men would sneak from behind the curtain and bash the guest's head in.

The women would cut the throat of the victim to make sure they were dead. Afterwards a trap door over the victim's chair will be opened and the body would be transported to the cellar for disposal. Once the body was in the cellar it would be ransacked with cash and other valuables stolen, undressed and buried somewhere on the property. A lot of the Bender's victims were found in the Orchard they kept. No clear motive as to why the Benders killed except for the thrill of it.

The killings weren't discovered until Dr. William Henry York went missing. His family organised a search party and questioned people along the trail. The Benders came under suspicion but it was suggested they wait for hard evidence before any steps could be taken. A town meeting was held, and it ended in a resolution that all the house would be searched.

Even though the Benders were under suspicion, surveillance was somehow overlooked, giving the Benders a chance to escape. Their disappearance wasn't even noticed until some days after. By then it was too late to track and capture the Benders. Their house was searched, and bodies of their victims were found.

The Benders were never definitively found.

Next time you complain about your family being odd, remember things could be much, much worse.

Chapter Eight: The Nefarious Nanny

Nothing is threatening about a woman who looks like your favourite granny. One who is always smiling. It was said that Nancy Hazel also known as Nannie Doss smiled all the way to prison. Even more  astonishing? She targeted people close to her, family members, where most serial killers targeted strangers that fit into their victim spectrum. Nannie Doss murdered her mother, grandson, four of her husbands, her sister and her mother in law.

Nannie Doss' early childhood was dominated by a harsh, abusive father who forced his children to work on his farm instead of going to school. At the age of 16, she got married to a colleague in the linen factory she worked. Her husband insisted on living with his mother who took most of his attention making Doss feel unneeded. The marriage ended. One of the earliest report suspicions of Doss was by her daughter Melvina who had just given birth. She thought she saw Doss stick a hat pin into her newly born baby's head. When she asked for confirmation from her family, nobody actually saw the hat pin go in. All they saw was Doss holding a pin after she'd told them the baby had died. The doctor was unable to pinpoint the exact cause of death. Melvina's other son Robert also died mysteriously while he was in Doss' care. The cause of his death was asphyxia from unknown causes. After his death, Doss received payment of $500 she took out on an insurance claim.

Her husband was the next to go. His name was Robert Franklin Harrelson. They got married shortly after meeting through a lonely hearts advertisement. The night before she killed him, he drank himself to stupor and raped Doss. The next day she found his jar of corn whiskey buried in the ground and mixed it with rat poison. Her next victim was her next husband, Arlie Lanning who she married just three days after she met him through another lonely hearts advertisement. She eventually killed him and his mother. Afterwards the house they shared together burned down and Doss pocketed the insurance money.

Nannie killed again, this time another husband, then her own mother. Wherever she went a frail of bodies seemed to follow her.

Suspicions finally came after she killed the fourth husband, Samuel Doss. He had been hospitalized in the early hour of the day for severe digestive tract infection. He was released from the hospital but Doss in a rush to collect insurance money killed him. Samuel Doss' doctor became suspicious and ordered an autopsy. During the autopsy, huge amounts of arsenic were found in Samuel's system leading to the verdict of murder.

Nannie Doss was quickly arrested and tried. Even though she confessed to her other murders, she was only tried for one. The state settled for life imprisonment instead of the death sentence because of her gender. Nannie Doss died of Lukemia on the 2nd of June, 1965. By then she had succeeded in killing almost everyone in her life.

Chapter Nine: The Monster Killer of China

He is China's most prolific serial killer. With a recorded 67 deaths to his name. His name was Yang Xinghai. Born on the 29th of July, 1968. He terrorized multiple states in China, breaking into houses, murdering and raping his victims.

Xinghai was born in Zhengyang County, Zhumadian, Henan Province, China to a low-income family where he was the last child. By 1988 he was already being sentenced to labour camps for crimes like rape and theft. By 1999 he had progressed to murder. He broke into people's home, the areas he terrorized were mostly populated by farmers. After breaking into their homes, he killed the occupants of the house with axes, shovels, hammers, always wearing new clothes and large shoes to disguise his identity.

The police arrested him after he acted suspiciously at a routine inspection of an entertainment centre. He was taken in for investigation and further questioning. It was discovered that he was wanted in four other provinces for murder. He admitted to 65

murders, twenty-three rapes and five serious assaults. His motives have been speculated on by the media who dubbed his the "Monster killer."

It has been suggested that some of the killings were carried out of hate for the society. Xinghai is even quoted to have said,

"When I killed people I had a desire. This inspired me to kill more. I don't care whether they deserve to live or not. It is none of my concern...I have no desire to be part of society. Society is not my concern."

He was a Sociopath who didn't play by the rules of society or even think they applied to him. He was found guilty by the court and killed by a firing squad. A fitting end to a life that brought so much violence with it.

Chapter Ten: The Red Ripper

This book started with the infamous and horrifying story of Jack the Ripper, a serial killer of Unknown identity who got away with it. It only fits to end the final chapter of the book with another who shared his name and was just as, if not even more brutal. Andrei Romanovich Chikatilo.

He was born on the 16th of October 1936, in a time of farming. His family barely had any food to eat and often had to resort to eating grass and leaves just to survive. Through out his life, he suffered from impotence, unable to either get or maintain an erection. This affected his relationship with females. His first admitted sexual assault was when he wrestled his younger sister's eleven year old friend to the ground and ejaculated on her.

Before his first recorded murder, he worked as a teacher in multiple schools. In these schools, he was fired after a while for molesting the students. He reportedly fondled himself in class. On one occasion he was in a pool with a female student, he swam towards her and grabbed her tightly while she struggled against him until he ejaculated. The assaults escalated into the rape and murder of more than 52 victims. All his adult victims were female and the children victims were a mix of both sexes.

His first recorded murder was on 22nd December 1978. He lured a young girl of 9

Yelena Zakotnova to a house which he had secretly purchased. There he tore off her clothes and attempted to rape her. He was unable to get an erection. When all his attempts failed, he strangled the girl and stabbed her three times, ejaculating as he stabbed her. Chikatilo was a sexual sadist, unable to achieve pleasure without the suffering of his victims. Though numerous bits of evidence linked Chikatilo to the murder, they were ignored and shortly after another man was tried for his crime. The man, Aleksandr Kravchenko was sentenced to prison for the crime and eventually executed.

After the first victim, The red ripper tried to keep his murderous urges in check but failed and succumbed to his dark desires again. This time he lured Larisa Tkachenko on the 3rd of September 1981 away from a public library with the pretext of drinking vodka and relaxing. As soon as they got to a secluded part of the woods,

Chikatilo tore off her clothes and tried to rape her. Mud was forced down her throat to stifle her screams. He couldn't get an erection and didn't have any knife on him, so instead he used his teeth and a stick to stab her, biting off her nipple. After the kill, he loosely covered her body in leaves, making it easy for her to be found the next day. This type of behaviour eventually became a pattern. After a brutal kill, there would be haphazard attempts made to conceal the body.

After that second kill, Chikatilo gave up on fighting his murderous urges. It was clear to him that the only way to achieve orgasm was through the mutilation and torture of women and children. He lured his victims away from public bus parks and train stations under multiple pretenses. It didn't seem to matter that he left a lot of DNA evidence around the frame scenes, police was incapable of finding the murderer. With a job that encouraged him to travel all over the Soviet Union, there was no shortage of victims to add to his body count. The brutality of the killings caused an uproar from the public and some high-ranking officials that tasked police to find the killer immediately.

Chikatilo was initially been arrested but was let go for lack of evidence, mainly after his blood tested type A but the DNA evidence the police had of semen was AB. After he was spotted leaving a crime scene discovered later, police investigated again and found out that though he had type A blood, his semen was type AB. The police had found their killer, but not before he was able to mutilate and end the lives of an alleged 56 plus persons.

On February 14th, 1994 Chikatilo was executed by a single gunshot wound behind his right ear. His quick death was nothing compared to the brutal, savage end he gave his victims.

Conclusion

Thank you again for purchasing this book! I hope this book took you on an exciting ride and was able to help you enter into the world of some of the world's worst serial killers for a little bit.

Finally, if you enjoyed this book, then I'd like to ask you for a favor, would you be kind enough to leave a review for this book? It'd be greatly appreciated!

Thank you and good luck!

www.ingramcontent.com/pod-product-compliance
Lightning Source LLC
Chambersburg PA
CBHW050707160426
43194CB00010B/2036